Some Pretty Crazy Things

EILEEN DISTASIO-CLARK

*With Great Love and Appreciation to Those Who
Have and Do Bless My Life.*

My Family:

*Joseph DeStasio Sr. & Miriam Lucille Baragone
DeStasio, My Late Parents.*

*Andrea Jean DeStasio McIntosh, My Older Sister
and Their Families.*

*Joseph DeStasio Jr., My Younger and Only Brother
and Their Families.*

*Donna Marie DeStasio Wagner, My Younger Sister
and Their Families.*

My Children:

Eileen, Rebekah, Rachel, S. Michael,

Jennifer, Sharon, Tara, Stephanie,

Apryll, Mikaelah, & M. Trevor

and THEIR Families!!

ACKNOWLEDGEMENTS

First and foremost, I express, deeply, my sincere gratitude to our Heavenly Father for blessing me with the gift and talent of writing! I know I could not do what I do without His assistance.

I also want to acknowledge and express gratitude to the members of my birth family—Joseph Sr., Miriam, Andrea, Joseph Junior, and Donna. All the experiences of my childhood years, experiences that taught me so very much and enabled me to reveal my true self to myself, came about through my experiences and relationships with them.

And, of course, it goes without saying, but I will say it anyway: I also want to acknowledge and note my gratitude to my children, Eileen, Rebekah, Rachel, S. Michael, Jennifer, Sharon, Tara, Stephanie, Apryll, Mikaelah, and M. Trevor, and their families! Through multiple things they said to me, over multiple years, I finally came to the realization that

Heavenly Father gave me the gift of writing and opened the doors to these experiences because He knew that by sharing them with others, others could feel His love too.

And He definitely wants us all to know that He, Heavenly Father, Heavenly Mother, and Jehovah truly do loves us!!!

INTRODUCTION

There are sixteen books in this series, which I refer to as *"The Ellie Series."* All of the characters in these stories portray real people from my life. The main characters depict the members of my family: Daddy is my daddy; Mommy is my mommy; Jeannie is my older sister; Junior is my brother; Maria is my younger sister, and Ellie is me. Now, those are not our actual first names, but they do reference us.

The first story in the series presents our Heavenly Father's Plan of Salvation and takes place in the Pre-Earth World. Now, of course, because we all—when we were born—received what is known as The Veil of Forgetfulness, I do not actually remember everything from or about the Pre-Earth World, but I do know about and understand it from much study and worship as a member of The Church of Jesus Christ of Latter-Day Saints, and memories restored to me through the Holy Spirit. So, from this story there is much truth to be learned.

The last story in the series is set in the Post-Mortal World, and presents a depiction of what happens to us after this life. Again, because I have not gone there yet, I cannot say I 'remember' this. But, I have also learned about the Post-Mortal World from much study and worship as a member of The Church of Jesus Christ of Latter-Day Saints.

All of the other stories are based on true events from my life; events that actually occurred when and how they are depicted in these stories. I chose these events because they are among the many occurrences in my life that presented—or revealed that which I already knew without having to be taught—Principles of Eternal Truths.

Also, I chose these events as the settings for my stories because they depict wonderful learning moments from my childhood and adolescent years, lessons that have blessed and benefited me throughout the whole of my life and will forever continue to do so. Also, through these great truths and their consequences in my life, I have been able to share them with many others, whose lives have also been blessed by them.

So, please, read and enjoy, then care and share the messages and stories with others!!

Now, there are also a couple of things you can look for:

In each story, the title of the previous story is presented in *italicized* form, the title of the next story is presented in *Capitalized Italicized* form, and the title of the story being read is presented in **emboldened** form.

Also, every story has at least one word that is uncommon or 'created.'

So, as you read, search, find, and have fun!

SOME PRETTY CRAZY THINGS

"What did you think you were doing?!" Mommy shouted with alarm as she ran up the attic stairs to Ellie's bedroom. Well, it was not just Ellie's bedroom; she shared it with her older sister Jeannie, but it was Ellie who had frightened Mommy, and that was why Mommy was running up to the attic bedroom, to make certain Ellie was okay and to find out why she had been doing something so crazy!

"Nothing," Ellie replied weakly, as she slowly dropped down onto her bed, "nothing... nothing... nothing..."

"Ellie!" Mommy responded, as she sat down on Jeannie's bed, which was across the room from Ellie's, "That answer will not do this time! I need an explanation and you are the only one who can give it to me. Now, tell me, what did you think you were doing?!"

***Uh, let me pause here, and explain something. Crazy things were not things one would not expect from Ellie. She always did crazy things, not that she thought they were crazy when she set out to do them, but needless to say, though I will say it anyway, it never took long for her to figure out what everyone

4

else could already see. How crazy those things were!***

'What kind of crazy things?' you may be wondering. Well, since I believe you are—and even if you are not—I will tell you what some of those crazy things were, but only just a few. If I were to try to tell you all the crazy things Ellie has done, you would be sitting there listening to me for the next... well... I guess I do not know exactly how long that would take, but I do know it would be a very long time. So, I will keep this short, and just share a few of them.

There was one time when the Stations—Ellie's family—was vacationing by the beach in Wildwood, New Jersey. In fact, that was one of their most favorite places to vacation. They all liked the cabin in which they stayed, which was right aside of the beach. They really enjoyed walking on the boardwalk every night. And, they absolutely loved playing on the beach every day! That was probably the most fun part of their vacation for... hmmm... probably all of them.

They would build sand castles, bury each other in the sand, hunt for seashells, and swim in the ocean. Now, most of the time, they stayed close to the shore and played in the water. When they did go into the water to swim, they almost never went far enough into the water for the water to be over their heads. But Ellie? Well, she was a curious sort and very much enjoyed exploring things, everything! So...

One time, Ellie and Junior had been playing in the water that only went up to their knees. They were having a great time jumping over the waves as they came up to the shore, splashing each other, and looking for shells. After a little while, which seemed like a long while to them, they decided they wanted to go farther out into the water and actually swim. So, they did.

Now, Junior still stayed close to the beach, but Ellie swam out farther and farther and fa... well, you get the idea. She not only swam out far enough for the water to be over her head, but she dove down into the water and swam underneath the waves. While she was under the water swimming, she found something she thought looked pretty interesting, so she picked it up and took it back to the beach.

As she swam to the beach, the 'thing' that she had picked up, by its 'umbrella head,' as she called it, wiggled and wriggled, squirmed and squiggled in her hand, and continued to so do as she walked up to the blanket where the rest of her family was lounging in the sun.

Now, Ellie had no idea what it was that she had found but, because she was totally captivated by it, there was excited interest in her voice when she called out to them, "Hey! Look what I found."

Much to her surprise, Mommy's reaction was one of alarm! "Ellie, where did you get that?" she yelled. "Drop it! Now!!"

And Daddy, as he jumped up and hustled toward Ellie, called out with just as much alarm, "What are you doing?!" When he was close enough to do so, he took from her hand what she had found, which, by the way, was a jellyfish, and threw it back into the water, well at least on the sand where the tides come in and wash everything back out to sea, which is exactly what happened to the jellyfish.

With obvious disappointment in her voice, Ellie asked, "Daddy, why did you do that?"

Taking her hand and walking with her back to the blanket, he asked her, "Ellie, do you know what that was?"

"Well, no," Ellie answered, "but I thought it was really cute, so I wanted to show it to everyone." Then she asked, "What was it?"

"It was a jellyfish," Daddy replied, "and, while not all jellyfish have stingers long enough to sting people, some of them do. That is why it is wise to leave them alone and stay away from them. I really do not know how you were even able to pick up that jellyfish and bring it back to shore with you, without being stung. But, Ellie, if it had stung you, we would be on our way to the hospital right now."

Ellie was stunned. "Oh!" she said, as she sat down on the sand, next to Maria—her little sister. "I had no idea!" Then, as she helped Marie build... whatever it was she was building in the sand, she thought about what Daddy had said and realized that God, once again, protected her. He had done that before... many times, and she was pretty sure He would do it again... many times. And, she was right!

In fact, one of those other times was one of the times that Ellie went out to take a walk, which was something she always loved to do—take walks! She had taken a book with her because another thing she loved to do was read. Now, anyone else would have walked to the park, or the trail along the riverside, or the playground, or... well, you get the idea. Anyone else would have taken him or herself somewhere where there were benches and then sat down to read.

Did Ellie do that? Nope! As she walked up Chestnut Street, she opened the book to the first page of the first chapter and began reading.

When she got to the corner, she turned right and continued down 3rd Avenue, across Cherry Street, and then across Franklin Street; all the while, rather than paying attention to where she was going or what was around her, she was reading her book. As she became more enrapt by... it was what her book was about, her steps, which had begun at her usual peppy pace, slowed down to an almost, sort of, just about what we could call a saunter. So deeply engaged in her book she was that she did not even seem to notice, or hear, the traffic as she approached Penn Avenue, which was the busiest street, and the main thoroughfare, in West Reading. Nope! She was not in tune with anything except her book until...

All of a sudden, as Ellie stepped off the curb onto Penn Avenue, a gazillion horns blared from the north, the south, the east, and the west, well, at least that is how it sounded, and tires screeched on both sides of Ellie, on her right and on her left, sounding like a screaming menagerie. Okay, so that might be a little bit exaggerated, but it did get her attention! In fact, so alarming was all the noise, that Ellie jumped as high as a hot-air balloon on its way to Australia! Well, okay, maybe not that high, but at least high enough to have dunked a ball into a hoop on a basketball court. Anyway, looking at all of the traffic that had piled up and seeing some not-so-happy expressions, Ellie closed her book, ran across the avenue, and jumped up onto the curb. Then she just continued to hustle, with a book in hand, on her way to... wherever she was going.

And as she was walking, this time with her book in her hand by her side, instead of in front of her face, she thought, *wow, I could have been hit by a car again, but I was not.* Then, looking up, in the direction of Heaven, she said, in a quiet, sincere voice, "Thank you!" knowing that God had protected her... again!

Now if that does not give you a good idea of how crazy the crazy things were that Ellie did, maybe this will.

Ellie's family always got together with their grandparents, aunts, uncles, and cousins for holidays.

Some holidays they spent with her daddy's family and some holidays they spent with her mommy's family. For some of the holidays, like Christmas, they got together at one of the grandparent's houses. On some of the other holidays, like Memorial Day, they got together at a park or a playground where there were picnic tables.

It was at one of their Memorial Day picnics, which they almost always—but not always, always—had at the West Reading Playground, that Ellie displayed her highly developed craziness! Ellie, her sisters, Jeannie and Maria, her brother, Junior, and several of their cousins were all playing on the swings. They were swinging as high as they could to see how high the highest swinger could swing. Now, most of them were being sensible and sitting on the seat of the swing. But Ellie? Was she sitting on the seat of the swing? Nope! Was she just watching the others swing? Nope! 'Well, what was she doing?' you may be wondering. Well, just in case you are, I will tell you. She was standing on the swing!

Yes, you read that right; she was standing on the seat of the swing, holding tight to the chains, as she swung forward and backward, and backward and forward, and fo... okay, so you know how she was swinging. Anyway, she had devised a plan that she was certain would provide all the momentum needed to get the swing as high as the swing could get!

"What was that plan," you are probably now asking.

Well, I will tell you what that plan was.

As she swung backwards, she bent her knees, 'stooping down,' so as to give her more upward momentum when she straightened her legs. And as she swung forwards, she bent her knees, 'stooping down,' so as to give herself more upward momentum when she straightened her legs. She continued, and continued, and cont... okay, okay, you know what she did, and it worked! Not only did she swing higher than all her siblings and cousins swung, but she also swung higher than the highest the swing should have been swung.

"Now, what do you mean by that?" You most likely want to know.

Well, again, I will tell you.

High enough was she swinging that the seat of the swing was level with the top of the swing-set bar. She thought it was awesome to be able to see over the swing-set, until...

Being in that position, horizontal with the top bar, made it rather difficult for her to keep a tight enough grasp on the chains. And her feet began to slip off the seat. About the second, or was it the third, maybe it was the fou... oh well, whatever time it was when she went up, her feet did slip off of the seat and, on her way down, she lost her grip. Needless to say—but I will say it anyway—she fell off the swing, landing on her back on the solid, tar-paved ground, and it was a hard landing!!!! Hard enough that she just laid there, motionless, which was so out of character for Ellie that everyone got scared. Even though most of them just stood stone still, looking at her, not knowing what to do, say, or think. Junior ran over to her, screamed her name several times, to which there was no response, and then ran up to the picnic tables where all the adults were, yelling loud enough to be heard on the other side of the world. Well okay, not heard that far away, but still, quite loudly, as loud as he could yell, "Ellie's dead! Ellie's dead!"

Of course, that got everyone's attention and, just as of course, Daddy and Mommy jumped up, like a kangaroo in a fight... well... not really like a kangaroo in a fight. But they most certainly did jump up in a flash, ran as fast as Tommie Smith ran to win the finals in the 1968 Summer Olympics, well, maybe not that fast, but superfast, none-the-less, being the first ones to get to Ellie.

Daddy knelt down beside Ellie, took her hand, and, with seriously concerned emotion, called her name, "Ellie! Ellie! Ellie!"

After the third call, Ellie slowly opened her eyes, looked up—as best she could—sat up with Daddy's help and then, in a quiet, whiney tone, asked, "What happened?" as she rubbed the back of her head.

As Daddy helped her up, Jeannie explained, with a bit of a scolding tone, "You fell off the swing. You wouldn't have if you had been sitting on the swing instead of standing on it."

"Are you okay?" Mommy asked with sincere concern.

"Yeah, I think so," Ellie said, as she walked, with help from everyone else, back up to the picnic tables, "but nothing looks... right, and my head sure does hurt! I guess that was a pretty crazy thing to do."

"Yeah!!!" Jeannie, Maria, Junior, and all the cousins replied emphatically.

"Why did you decide to do that?" Mommy asked, fully believing that she knew what Ellie's reason was.

"Well, I had told everyone that that was the best way to swing the highest, but no one believed me. So, I had to show them and... and... *I had to prove myself.*"

Naturally, there was a full chorus of "Oh, Ellie" groans to be heard, but everyone was genuinely concerned for her. That was why they all decided instead of having the kids go back to the swings; they would all stay at the picnic tables and play some board games while the picnic lunch was finishing to cook.

It was Daddy who volunteered to go to the car to get some games, and he asked Ellie to help him. Of course, she said yes; there was nothing Ellie would not do with Daddy. After picking out three games— Monopoly, Bingo, and *A Deck of Cards*—Daddy and Ellie walked back to the picnic tables.

On their way back, Daddy told Ellie, "Do not forget to thank God for taking care of you. With as far as you fell, onto the hard tar-paved pavement, you could have been very seriously hurt, but apparently you were not."

Now, I could go on and on and on and... okay, you know what I am saying, so I will just go on, or should I say back, to where we began.

"Ellie, why were you on the roof?!" Mommy demanded to know. "What were you doing?"

"Well," Ellie began as she pulled herself up to a sitting position and turned to face Mommy. "I thought it was a good idea. You see, I wanted to get a suntan."

"You?! You wanted to get a suntan?!" Mommy questioned with great surprise. Bathing in the sun was not something Ellie, in all fifteen years of her life, to that, had ever been interested in. In fact, she always thought it was ridiculous to lay out in the sun. "Why? When did you change your feelings about tanning?" Mommy continued.

"Well, I... I cannot say I really did change my feelings," Ellie began. "I think it is boring to just lay there, doing nothing. And I really do not want my skin to be a different color than what it is; I like the way I look. But... well... oh, I do not know. I think..."

Ellie paused. As she did, Mommy, after studying the expression on Ellie's face, asked, "Ellie, were you wanting to tan just because Jeannie does and your cousins and friends do?"

Ellie was quiet for a few moments. Well, it was a bit more than just a few, but it was not too long before she said, "I do not know, Mommy, maybe."

"Ellie," Mommy said as she arose from Jeannie's bed, walked over to Ellie, sat down beside her and put her arm around her, "you do not have to do what others do if it is not something you really want to do. In fact, it is better if you do not do anything just because others are doing it. You need to make your own choices and make them for the right reasons."

After giving Ellie a pretty little "big hug," Mommy also said, "And, I agree with you; suntanning is not desirable." Then, as Mommy headed for the stairs, before starting down, she turned to face Ellie and said, "Now, Ellie, if you do decide that you want to tan, DO NOT go out on the roof to do it! You do know what could have happened to you! Think about that!"

'Think about what?' you are probably wondering. Well, I will clear up that wonderment for you, by telling you what actually happened, why Ellie's mommy got so alarmed. In fact, you can step back in time with me, and we can "watch" what happened.

It was a warm, well maybe hot, early summer day, and Ellie was sitting in her room, her attic bedroom, trying to make her decision. She wanted to, but she did not want to. She thought, 'Well, maybe it will be fun,' but she also thought, 'I think I would hate it.' Then, she asked herself, "Well, where would I do that?"

Are you wondering what she was wondering if she should do and where she would do it? You probably are and I suppose you just want me to tell you. So, I will.

Ellie was sitting on her bed, looking out the window on the back side of her room, her attic bedroom, wondering if she wanted to try sunbathing. Now, do not misunderstand; it is not that Ellie had never had a tan; she most definitely did. She tanned really easily, so all she ever had to do was just be outside and unless she was fully covered with clothing, she got a tan.

Now, she did not really like getting a tan for a couple of reasons. One, she liked the way her skin looked, so she did not want to change that with a tan. Two, she did not like having tan lines, but of course, there was NO WAY, ABSOLUTELY NO WAY, she would ever tan with nothing on. Three, it was boring to just lay on the ground, doing nothing.

Oh! Wait! I said there were a couple of reasons and a couple is only two; I gave you three. Oh, well, at least you now understand why Ellie did, or should I say does, not like to tan. Nevertheless, there she was, sitting on her bed in pouting posture, wondering if she wanted to 'try it.' *After all,* she thought, *everyone else does it.*

Finally, after what seemed to be a millennium, or two, or three, or fo... okay, you know what I am saying; after a while, what seemed to be quite a while, at least to Ellie, who was usually a 'spur-of-the-moment' decision maker, she made her decision to try tanning. But where would she do that? She really did not want to lie on the ground in the yard where all the neighbors could see her. Besides, if she did that because their Catalpa tree shaded most of the yard, she would have to lie on the pavement and that would not be comfortable.

So, where should I go? she thoughtfully questioned. Then, the idea came to her. She would lie out on the roof—the roof over the back side of their house, which was lower than the roof that covered their attic, which was her room—well, hers and Jeannie's. The back window in their room opened up to the back roof, so it would be very easy to just step out onto the roof.

After changing into her swimsuit and grabbing a large towel, she opened the window and climbed out onto the roof. She spread the towel out on the roof in front of the window, laid down on it, and... well, she did nothing! She just laid there, in the sun, which was quite hot. It definitely felt much more hot on the roof than it did on the ground. And that was not good, at least not for Ellie.

After a while—a not too long while—she began to feel... funny... light-headed... not good. She was even beginning to have a hard time getting a good breath. So, she decided to go back in. She got up, picked up the towel, and started to walk. But what she did not realize was that the direction she was walking in was not the direction that would take her back to the window; it was the direction that would take her to the edge of the roof and, if she kept walking when she got there... well, you get the idea.

For some reason that even Mommy did not know, Mommy was outside, right aside from the house, directly below the part of the roof that Ellie was walking on. For some reason, even though there was no reason for her to do it, she looked up, just as Ellie was nearing the edge of the roof and saw Ellie walking toward the edge of the roof. She could tell that Ellie did not know what she was doing, so, faster than it takes a peregrine falcon—the fastest flying bird of them all, to fly from one tree to the next, and louder than the Republic XF-84H Thunderscreech airplane, the loudest of all airplanes—Mommy screamed, "Ellie, go back! Go Back!! GO BACK!!! Turn around, Ellie!!!! Do NOT take another step!!!!! TURN AROUND AND GO THE OTHER WAY!!!!!!"

Somehow, even though Ellie did not seem to be conscious of what was happening, she must have heard her mommy because she turned around, walked slowly in the direction that took her to the window, and fell into her room—literally!!! She slowly pulled herself up and sauntered over to her bed as her mommy came running up the steps.

Now, knowing that you know the rest of the story, I will just stop there. But there is one thing I must add.

As Ellie propped her pillow up against the wall that her bed was positioned in front of and leaned back on her pillow, she thought about what her mommy had said, "You do know what could have happened to you! Think about that!"

It took no effort and even less time than it takes to take a breath for Ellie to realize what her mommy meant. If she had taken just one more step... well, let me just say this. If she had taken that one more step, it would have been her one last step, and Ellie probably would have been looking down from Heaven after that step.

Again, Ellie knew that God took care of things! He stepped in and saved her, and He did so through her mommy. As she thought about that, how God often works through some people to help other people, she made the decision—one that she would never go back on—to be the kind of person through whom God could work, even if that meant she had to stop doing **some pretty crazy things**. Now, of course, she also knew that it was very unlikely that she would ever really be able to stop all of those crazy things because that was just who she was, but she also knew that she could always rely upon God to take care of her!

ABOUT THE AUTHOR

Eileen DiStasio-Clark is the second oldest of four children. She is the mother of eleven children and grandmother to twenty-three grandchildren, to date. As a member of The Church of Jesus Christ of Latter-Day Saints, she serves in various positions, teaching, leading, and ministering to children, youth, and adults. Currently, she is also a Family History Missionary. Eileen established the Pursuit of Excellence Institute of Family Education, a non-profit organization focused on strengthening the family. Presently she holds an AA, a BA, and an MA in Clinical Psychology and is working on the completion of her Doctoral Degree.